GEOMORPHOLOGY – THE AGES OF ETERNITY

The Drakensberg mountains had their origin some 200-million years ago when a vast land mass known as Gondwanaland existed. Through aeons of time, water streaming down from higher ground collected and formed a huge swamp where dinosaurs and other prehistoric creatures roamed... Then came a time of extreme aridity, of dust storms and desert, killing off all that had lived in these steaming swamplands.

About 160-million years ago Gondwanaland ceased to exist – rent asunder by catastrophic eruptions: Molten lava poured from fissures and across the wastelands to a height of 1500 metres... and eventually gradually cooled. Then yet another cataclysm occured and the continents of Africa, South America, Australasia and Antartica were created. In Africa, climate and erosion took its toll ...and about 145-million years of weathering has formed the Drakensberg of today. The Molteno, and Red bed layers – the bottom of the original swamp, and the sands of the Desert era can be seen in many of the Little 'Berg's rock faces – together with the hard volcanic basalt on top.

CLIMATE AND VEGETATION

The climate of the Drakensberg is predominantly one of warm to hot summer days – with fairly regular afternoon thunderstorms – and cool nights: Also spells of mist and drizzle can be experienced.

Winter days are mainly mild to warm, and dry, except during an occasional passing 'cold front' which often brings snow to the peaks: Nights can be cold to very cold; with frost.

Altitude and topography, together with changing pressure systems over the sub-continent play a significant climatic role.

The high altitude of the Drakensberg areas (1500 – 3000 m) will determine the lower temperatures and humidity – in comparison to those of the coastal plains.

Vegetation is influenced by height and relative position: At higher levels there are heaths and grasses – whilst in the valleys and lower foothills one sees dense indigenous forests and grasslands. South-facing slopes by limiting sunshine enables moisture to be retained, thus producing greater and lusher plant growth.

THE ROYAL NATAL NATIONAL PARK REGION

When viewed from the Tugela Valley, The Amphitheatre, with its 4 km wall of weathered precipices has the prominent Sentinel (3165 m) on the right hand side: Next to it is Beacon Buttress (3121 m) where Lesotho, Natal and Qwa Qwa meet, and on the left is the 3047 m high Eastern Buttress. Mont-aux-Sources (3282 m), is situated about 3 km from the escarpment's edge. It is on this plateau, known as Pofung (place of the Eland) by the Sotho people, that the Tugela River begins its long journey to the Indian Ocean. Four other major rivers also have their origins near here – two of which the Eastern and Western Khubedu, eventually join the mighty Orange River to flow into the South Atlantic Ocean some 2190 km away to the west.

Early Europeans must have first visited this northern area in the 1840's... with Dr. Matthews doing a great deal of exploring and climbing here in 1870 – and leaving us one of the first recorded accounts of a climb to the top, and of a visit to the Cannibal Caverns where a tribe of Africans had had to resort to cannibalism after the ravages of the warrior chief Chaka and his impis.

In 1878 a young English governess and her farmer husband spent a honeymoon camped by their ox-wagon in the Tugela River valley not far from the Gorge. At night they could hear the cries of wild animals – and whilst out exploring one day were even to come across a group of Bushmen who must have been among the last remaining of these Stone Age hunters in the Drakensberg – whom she was to describe as being 'weird-looking creatures hardly bigger than a child of ten'.

Not long afterwards sounds of wood-chopping and sawing were to fill these wooded valleys when the colonial government granted concessions, to such men as Dooley, for the cutting down of tall yellowwood trees – an exceptionally strong timber used in the building of homesteads and wagons.

In 1903 Walter Coventry bought the farm 'Goodoo' and his farmhouse was to become part of a hostel in 1913; three years later, the National Park was established with Coventry as its First Warden.

In 1930 two 100-rung chain ladders were installed to provide easier access to the Amphitheatre's plateau – where many an 'old' climber will nostalgically remember the well-kept mountain hut.

The old hotel burnt down in 1941... and was rebuilt in time for the Royal visit of 1947, when the 'Park' and 'Hotel' acquired the title 'Royal' – and it was during this year that the Natal Parks Board was formed.

The Natal Parks Board has continued to maintain a high standard in its conservation and wildlife preservation – by the control of such aspects as soil erosion, eradication of non-indigenous plants, and poaching etc.

There is a useful booklet, available at the park, on all the walks and climbs – though the walk to the Gorge is one that should not be missed. The scenery on this walk becomes progressively more dramatic and picturesque as one nears the actual gorge – with the spectacular view of Devil's Tooth and Eastern Buttress being a rewarding sight at the end of the 8 km walk.

There are several holiday resorts in the area – each with its individual character, charm, and scenery – and conveniently situated to the Park.

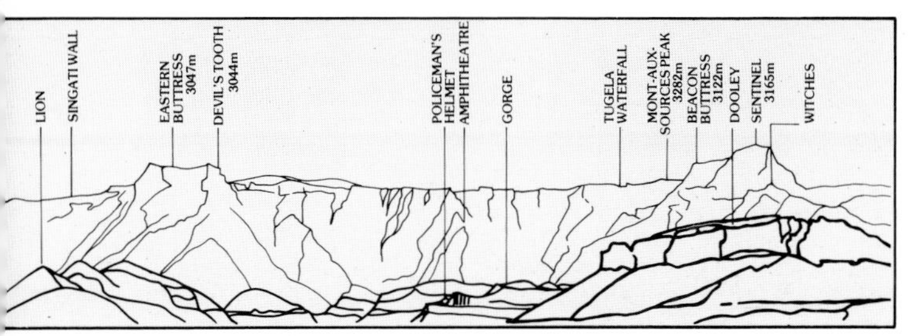

Story of a River... The Tugela

The Tugela River begins its life above the Amphitheatre plateau on the slopes of Mont-aux-Sources (3278 m) – where marshes formed by the upper escarpment's high rainfall (over 1500 mm per annum), feed a little bubbling stream. In mid-summer this stream will have grown into a small river by the time it reaches the edge of the Amphitheatre wall, from where it will plunge as the Tugela Falls some 850 m in five vertical drops into the gorge far below – making it one of the highest waterfalls in the world. From about May to September the stream on top freezes over sufficiently to stop the flow of water over the lip, and the Tugela has then to be content in beginning its course as a river among the masses of boulders in the gorge.

Here in 'The Gorge', our river has through the ages created some most spectacular scenery – having carved steep and dramatic ravines with precarious rock and grassy slopes above the boulder-strewn river bed. The vegetation, in keeping with the high rainfall, is lush – with an abundance of trees, smaller plants, and grasses. Just before meeting the Devil's Tooth Gully, the Tugela has gouged a remarkable sandstone tunnel some 40 metres long with tall, leaning sides which appear to meet and form this 'tunnel'. The scenery in this vicinity is outstanding – with rocky spires and peaks visible all round.

From here the river continues downwards through a gully with vertical north-facing sandstone cliffs and densely afforested opposite banks; it is at this point that one can observe a good example of Molteno, Red Beds and Sandstone strata; as described in the geomorphology section.

...The terrain soon broadens, and the Tugela widens – as it is joined by other rivers and streams on its long meandering journey through Natal... and on to its estuary at the Indian Ocean some 322 km away.

WINTER

Snow has been known to fall on the Drakensberg mountains, every month of the year – though a fall during the summer months is most unusual. In winter on the High Berg, the heavier snowfalls can reach a depth of as much as two metres in the gullies and south-facing slopes... where it can last for several weeks ...whilst lower in the Little Berg snow disappears within a few days. Though temperatures on top of the mountain escarpment can drop as low as -15°C in winter, most holiday resorts experience a mild climate due to their protected positions in the shelter of valleys and lower slopes.

During most winters, between the months of May and September, one can usually anticipate some three to ten heavy snow falls on the 'berg. These falls with accompanying cold weather are most often preceeded by a few days of really warm weather. Most snow falls occur during early and late winter with mid-winter being usually dry.

(Opposite page) An aerial view showing the flat-topped Eastern Buttress (3047 m), with the slender column of the Devil's Tooth; and the Inner Tower in the foreground, with the Amphitheatre plateau which recedes into the background – linking up with Beacon Buttress (3121 m) and the Sentinel (3165 m) with the Maluti mountains of Lesotho in the distance.

(Top left) Climbers atop Beacon Buttress look across the Amphitheatre towards Eastern Buttress and Devil's Tooth.

(Far left) On the path to the top of the Amphitheatre – with the Sentinel in the background.

(Left) The northern slopes of the Amphitheatre showing the Sentinel, the 'Gully' and the traverse to the top.

The Witsieshoek mountain road (via Qwa Qwa) is a worthwhile drive, with a spectacular side view of The Amphitheatre and its peaks: Also the Maluti mountains, and the distant plains of Natal. The road attains a height of 2600 m and ends near the sheer base of the Sentinel: From here one can take a short but strenuous walk to the top of the Amphitheatre. This walk presents, relatively speaking, a very easy access to the top of the escarpment – but one should take careful note of the climbing tips in this booklet.

All of the Drakensberg's foothills are most suitable for horse-riding, walking and climbing, trout fishing etc; and the hotels and resorts all make the most of these assets and natural attractions.

ROYAL NATAL NATIONAL PARK

★★TYYY

This comfortable, fully-licensed hotel is set amidst some of the Drakensberg's finest scenery – with many delightful walks close by. The hotel offers its guests most amenities including Bowls, Tennis, Horse-riding, Swimming and Fishing. Both this berg resort and the national park derived the title from the visit of the British Royal Family to this picturesque region in 1947.

Write to: P.O. Box Mont-aux-Sources 3353.
Telephone: (03642) and ask for Mont-aux-Sources No. 1.

Mont-aux-Sources Hotel

★TYYY

The Drakensberg's most scenically situated holiday resort – overlooks the impressive grandeur of the Amphitheatre, and enjoys superb views of the surrounding mountains. Adjoining the Royal Natal National Park, renowned for its walks and climbs – the hotel is known for its bowls tournaments, riding and fishing etc. – and for the friendly atmosphere of its ladies bar.

Write to: Private Bag 1, Mont-aux-Sources Natal 3353
Phone: (03642), ask for Mont-aux-Sources No. 7.

The CAVERN

"Holiday Resort of many happy returns"

Offers guests comfortable thatched accommodation in a sheltered valley of woods and waterfalls – surrounded by towering mountains. Where early Bushmen had once discovered this secluded Paradise...the Carte family has created a unique family resort known for its pleasant, friendly atmosphere; with fun activities for all.

"The Cavern" Private Bag X1626, Bergville 3350.
Telephone: (03642) 172.

Little Switzerland ★TYYY

Situated in a rugged mountainous countryside, this hotel with its peaceful atmosphere and panoramic vistas – has beautifully furnished thatched cottages set amongst gardens and lawns. The holiday resort is fully licensed, has all the conference facilities and guests can enjoy riding, bowls, tennis and swimming etc. Under the personal supervision of the owner.

Write to Private Bag X1661, Bergville 3350, Natal.
Telephone: (03642) and ask for Robbers Roost No. 2.

Sandford Park Lodge

Member of Club Caraville (AA recommended)

Our century-old lodge and coachhouse in the foothills of the Drakensberg is set in 100 acres of wooded countryside – and by catering for only some sixty guests ensures that personal attention with individual service; whilst providing every recreation to suit all the family. This farm-style retreat is ideally close to all the region's many scenic attractions.

Write: P.O. Box 7, Bergville 3350. Phone: (03642) '61'
Central Res: (011) 7066732 or 7065956; (031) 7014156

Hlalanathi

DRAKENSBERG RESORT

Overlooking the Tugela River – with its magnificent views of the Amphitheatre. This resort can accommodate 50 caravans/camp sites, and we also have self contained accommodation. For your enjoyment there is a swimming pool, braai, picnic places, and organized entertainment.

Telephone: (03642) 1812
Write to P.O. Box X1621, Bergville 3350.

NATAL PARKS BOARD

Reservations Officer:- P.O. Box 662, Pietermaritzburg 3200

Tendele Hutted Camp which looks out onto the Amphitheatre has accommodation consisting of thirteen bungalows and two cottages. There is also the **Mahai Camp Site** which is not far from the Royal Natal National Park Hotel and is next to the Mahai stream in well-wooded grounds. **Rugged Glen Nature Reserve** has camping facilities, and the Parks Board's stables are situated near here.

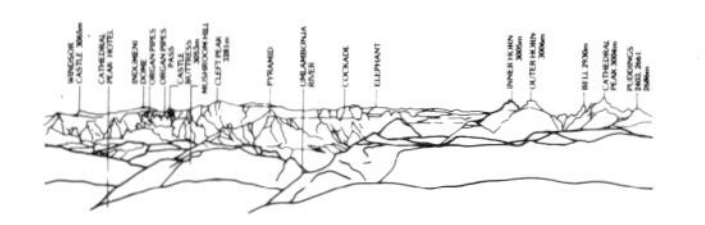

CATHEDRAL PEAK REGION

The beauty of Cathedral Peak Hotel's setting owes a great deal to its superb position looking out onto a ridge of mountains known as the Cathedral Spur. This massive spur which juts out at right angles from the main 'berg has at its north end the Three Puddings; with Cathedral Peak (3004 m), the first large free-standing peak, and the Bell (2930 m) next to it: Then the Outer and Inner Horns, Chessmen, Mitre and The Twins.

Looking southwards the long slopes of Cleft Peak (3281 m) are most prominent with the Organ Pipes and Ndumeni Dome (3206 m) to the left. The Column, and Pyramid are part of a small spur that strikes out from Cleft Peak – but are not readily visible as such due to their side view against the main 'berg.

This part of the Drakensberg was one of the last to be developed... when Philip van der Riet bought the farms 'Inhoek' and 'Schaapkraal' in 1937 with the intention of building a hotel in this beautiful setting.

It was long before this however, in 1847, that a mission station was founded in the area – and still exists today some 20 km away from the hotel. Woodcutters and hunting parties came to these foothills about 1910 – followed by farmers who were, by 1918, using the lands for grazing.

The upper valleys and slopes of these foothills continued as farms for many years, until 1938 when a Forest Research Station was established and plantations of pine were later set out – primarily to determine the ecological effect of the possible afforestation of this region. During this time Philip's son, Albert, had selected the site for Cathedral Peak Hotel overlooking the Umlambonja River and beneath the Cathedral Spur: By Christmas 1939 the hotel was ready to receive its first guests.

For many years Cathedral Peak was known as Zikhali's Horn – after the son of Matiwane. Matiwane was killed by Dingaan – Zikhali's life having been spared – he then fled and took refuge in Swaziland... where he fell in love with one of King Sobuza's many daughters. Later, they returned and settled in the Cathedral Peak area after bringing together again the scattered remnants of the original Amangwane tribe. The Swazi influence can still be seen along the country roads, in the design of their homes and in the tall thatch grass screens at the kraal entrances.

The walks and climbs in this area vary from easy strolls – to longer walks for the more energetic – to strenuous climbs for the really fit. Walks to the Tryme Trout Hatchery, Doreen Falls, or some river pool on the Umlambonja River are easy and well worthwhile – whilst a day trip to the Rainbow Gorge is most rewarding for those who appreciate beautiful indigenous forests and riverine scenery ... culminating in the narrow gorge itself with its two gigantic wedged boulders.

The climb up Cathedral Peak has probably been accomplished by more people than any other with 'there-and-back' taking a full day – as does the Cleft Peak climb which must rate as being one of the most outstanding in the 'berg where the views from the summit – across the numerous spurs... and further... are unsurpassed for majestic beauty.

The Cathedral Peak region has some of the most rewarding climbs in the Drakensberg. Unlike most of the 'berg, the Cathedral Spur and others which protrude from the main 'berg combine to create a more rugged and mountainous appearance.

These scenes show the distant Cathedral Spur from the side of Ndumeni Dome: 'Roland's Cave'; and an unusual spire in the Organ Pipes Pass.

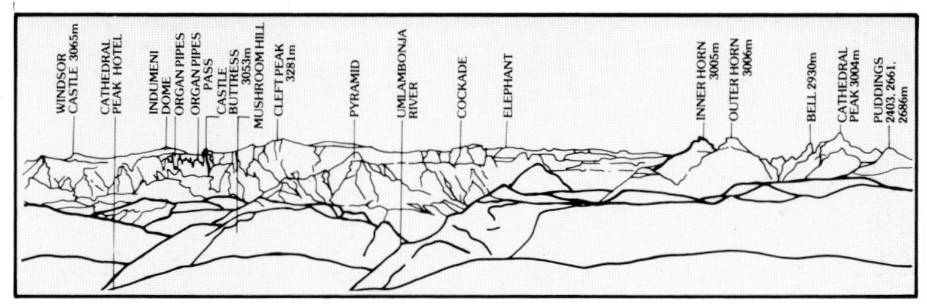

From the foothills of the Cathedral area one has a wonderful feeling of being surrounded by mountains – due to the Cathedral spur that extends out from the main 'berg at an acute angle. This physical feature is not immediately apparent – as the continuation of the main 'berg, behind this spur, is not visible from the front.
This surrounding of mountains has more than its share of beautiful features – of crags and spires, foothills, eroded sandstone shapes, mountain streams, rivers and pools.

Mushroom Rock – an apt name for this natural cave sandstone rock formation. The Drakensberg has many an example of this type of weathering where the softer sandstone – created from the desert era of 165-million years ago – has been eroded leaving behind the harder basalt top layer. 'Mushroom Rock' is a walk of about one and a half hours from the hotel.

Cleft Peak forms a solid unbroken rock wall background to a party of horseriders – with the Cathedral Peak Hotel in the foreground. Cleft Peak at 3281 m is one of the highest points on the main Drakensberg Escarpment. Behind the hotel is Tarn Hill. Mushroom Rock is situated at the point where the lower 'rock band' begins on the right hand spur between sun and shadow: In the left background can be seen the two humps of the Camel – with the vertical ridges of the Organ Pipes directly behind: The Ndumeni Dome is obscured by cloud.
The mountain pool is on the walk to Rainbow Gorge.

"THE EVERLASTING FIRSTS"

In 1836 two French missionaries, crossing a wind-swept plateau in northern Basutoland, climbed the slopes of a nearby hill – and named it Mont-aux-Sources (3282 m) because at that point they could see the source of five rivers: From there, they moved on... and reached the brink of a massive wall of rock – which today we know as The Amphitheatre: From this escarpment they gazed down into a land of mountains, rivers and valleys – Natal.
Fifty two years later, the first mountaineers in the Natal Drakensberg were the Stocker brothers – together they tackled Champagne Castle (3377 m) and eventually reached the summit: Many of the early climbers in the 'berg were not only to achieve ever-lasting acclaim in having been the first to reach the top – but some were also to earn the reputation of being really colourful characters. One such person was Tom Casement, a rumbustious Irish inn-keeper who besides being a climber of note in conquering the peaks of the Eastern Buttress (3047 m), Sentinel (3165 m) and The Amphitheatre (2972 m) – also earned the dubious honour of possessing a fiery vocabulary that was appallingly rich, ripe and ever ready! How he and pious Father Kelly were ever able to be companions in the same climbing party that reached the top of Cathkin Peak (3149 m) in 1912 can surely only be attributed to the hardy padre's partial deafness!

In the period of the 1930's and into the War years of 1939 – 1945, there were many magnificent rock climbers of the calibre of Brian Godbold, Doyle Liebenberg, Maurice Sweeney and "Snib" his wife, and Martin Winter etc, who between them were to conquer some twenty-five of the berg's most difficult summits. Each mountaineer has an individual style and technique embodying considerable stamina and courage: Some are reserved and softly-spoken: Others, even after a day's hard climbing, can still sing songs of the mountains and mountaineers... long into the night.
In the hundred years and more since those missionaries had discovered Mont-aux-Sources, there have been many noteworthy climbers and well-known characters – to single out *one* from such a formidable array of great climbers is doubtless an affrontery to the achievements of such intrepid men and women: However in so doing, it may well be an epitome of what men will dream of... and what some are also able to realise.

One such man who deserves a mention is George Thomson: A New Zealander who came to Natal... and stayed to climb its most difficult peaks. This extra-ordinary Kiwi bricklayer's ascent of 'The Column' in 1945 is an epic of determination and sheer skill in conquering, *freehand and without any climbing aid or rope*, a rock face described as being "... the most difficult peak in the Union" – and unlikely ever to be climbed. Yet if that was an epic, the conquest of Mponjwana (3085 m) must remain as the classic in achievement. George and Ken Snelson in their ascent had to carry out the most difficult traverses; work their way through numerous narrow chimneys; climb vertical slabs of sheer rock face with only small fingerholds to grip on to; surmount dreaded overhangs ... and finally rely on one vital boulder remaining firm when taking their weight – otherwise they would have hurtled down a horrifying 500 metres to certain death. Fortunately that boulder held... and the traditional cairn of stones to indicate their success was a lonely witness to one of the most remarkable climbs ever experienced.

What more typical of such a great climber than that his last climb should be the Outer Mnweni Pinnacle classified as a 'G' climb, and regarded as being almost unclimbable.

To most, George Thomson remains a legend; to some he has been judged as having been too impetuous and reckless: Yet by his achievements he proved he could climb alone, he could climb without a rope, he could climb...

"Great things are done when men and mountains meet –" William Blake

George Thomson (centre) with climbing friends at Cathedral Peak.
(Above left): 'The Column' and 'Pyramid'. George Thomson climbed 'The Column' (2929 m) solo in 1945. This individual feat, accomplished without rope, on this very dangerous peak, has never been repeated.
Brian Godbold, *(Top Right)*, an extremely proficient 'early' rock climber with more Drakensberg 'firsts' to his name than any other person.
(Above): George Thomson, at left, wearing the hat he sometimes wore when out on an 'easy' climb. Martin Winter, right, another most outstanding rock climber, who achieved numerous outstanding 'firsts' – and has taken part in many mountain rescues.

from my experience...

REG PEARSE has lived and climbed in the Drakensberg for over forty years: He writes with authority about these mountains he loves – and his book "Barrier of Spears" is a classic of factual 'berg experiences, and interesting local history.

I believe that familiarity with wild open country, and a love of the great outdoors, is vital if we wish to maintain, and improve the quality of life. Wilderness areas hold a special physical and spiritual value which are beyond price: But the unspoilt outdoors should never be taken for granted. They should be approached with due respect – and an appreciation of their potential dangers recognised. By observing these important factors – a world of joy and quiet delight awaits you.

Here is a summary of some of the precautions to be observed – together with a few tips I have learned in the Drakensberg over the years.

- *Plan your mountain climb well beforehand: Obtain one of the many excellent maps available, and a good compass, and always start your journey early in the day.*
- *Equip yourself adequately. Remember to include warm clothing and rain clothes. Blizzard conditions on the upper escarpment can blow up with startling suddenness – even in summer. Many experienced climbers carry a lightweight tent – even when their destination is to a known cave. A down-sleeping bag is important, especially in winter. Always carry more food than you think you'll require – taking careful consideration of each article's weight. Important items of your equipment are boots... never attempt a long hike with a brand new pair: Always ensure you have worn them in first. Wear two pairs of socks – a thin pair next to the skin, and the thicker ones over them.*
- *Always remember to complete destination details in the Mountain Register when setting off on long hikes; and to take your passport with you if venturing to the summit.*
- *Familiarise yourself with the High 'Berg gradually, and do your initial trips with an experienced climber. Never climb by yourself – a climbing party should ideally consist of three people.*
- *There are only 12 – 15 well-known mountain passes breaching the 100 km of rock wall between Mont-aux-Sources... and Giant's Castle. Take special note of where your nearest pass is – especially once you're on the top. Mist or snow can quickly obscure your route.*
- *Learn to interpret cloud formations, winds, and those signs that accompany a change in the weather. Remember that Drakensberg weather can change dramatically within a few minutes.*
- *Should you get caught out on the summit in thick mist it is often better to 'stay where you are', unless you are on a clearly-defined path, since it is extremely easy to become disorientated: With snow, it is better, if possible to get down off the escarpment since snow can sometimes continue falling for days – with the passes becoming choked up with ice and snow. If you are not near a pass it is important to do ones best to seek shelter behind a rocky outcrop, out of the wind. If completely lost, with food running short, one should head eastwards, following the course of a stream, if one is in the Little 'Berg. If on the summit of the main escarpment, head westwards, again down a stream bed.*
- *In summer especially, lightning can be a hazard. Keep away from high ridges, rock outcrops, overhangs, trees and fences. If you are on horseback, dismount and move away. Your best plan is to sit and wait for the storm to abate.*
- *In the event of your being in open country with a runaway grass fire advancing at speed towards you, head for either a nearby forested kloof, or a large area of bare rock. If you can't do this, then ignite the veld around you and step into this burnt area. This will then protect you. If all else fails, run right into the fire,... through it,... and then roll over to smother any flames from your clothing: Never try to run away from a fire unless you are quite sure you can make it to safety.*
- *If you are camping out on the summit, keep a sharp look out for thieves! They might well steal your ruck-sack, boots and gear.*
- *Never make camp in the bed of a river or stream – a flash flood can come upon you at great speed.*

How to deal with Snake-Bites

The majority of snakes in the Drakensberg are harmless, the exceptions being the Rinkhals, the Puff Adder, and the Berg Adder. The bite of the latter, however, is not known to be fatal.
The Rinkhals is a large snake, about a metre long. Colour is variable, but is usually dark brown to black, with whitish grey bands across the throat. Like the cobras, it will rear up and extend its hood when angry.
The Puff Adder is a slightly smaller snake, wide in girth, and up to 90 cm long. It has a large diamond-shaped head and a brown patterned design on its back. Because of its sluggishness it will rarely move out of your way as you approach.
The Berg Adder is smaller still, about 50 to 60 cm in length. Colour is from greyish olive to dark brown, with black markings. The golden rule in the case of all snake-bites is DO NOTHING, but get the victim to a doctor as quickly as possible. Don't run, and do not attempt to administer snake-bite serum.
In the case of a Rinkhals bite it is permissable to apply a tourniquet above the wound, but it must be loosened after half an hour...for about 30 seconds...thereafter a 20 minute tourniquet with 30 second loosening ...and finally 3 × 10 minute tightenings (with ½ minute intervals) – before removing the tourniquet completely.

WITH ALL SNAKE-BITES, IT IS ESSENTIAL TO RECEIVE MEDICAL ATTENTION AS SOON AS POSSIBLE.

CHAMPAGNE CASTLE – CATHKIN PEAK REGION

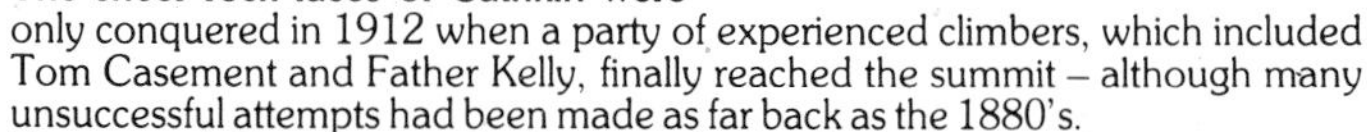

Cathkin Peak (3149 m) is by far the most prominent feature in this region; though not as high as Champagne Castle at 3377 m, which is partially hidden by the bulk of Cathkin – with Monk's Cowl (3234 m) completely obscured by this massive free-standing, flat-topped mountain.

The sheer rock faces of Cathkin were only conquered in 1912 when a party of experienced climbers, which included Tom Casement and Father Kelly, finally reached the summit – although many unsuccessful attempts had been made as far back as the 1880's.

The top of Champagne Castle is easily reached after a strenuous hike up Gray's Pass: Like Mont-aux-Sources, Champagne Castle was also long thought to be the highest point in South Africa – though a short distance southwards both eNjasuthi Dome (3410 m) and Mafadi (3446 m), bordering on Lesotho, are higher.

Sterkhorn (2973 m) the prominent peak to the right of Cathkin is also known as Mount Memory, having been adopted by the MOTH organisation in 1947 as a National War Memorial.

The first Europeans to this region were the Voortrekkers, during 1837 . . . then came the British settlers – one of the first being David Gray in 1855.

Shortly afterwards, as had happened in other 'berg regions, the woodcutters were to make their appearance. Bushmen were of course the first humans in the area, with the Ndedema Gorge to the north being practically a gallery of their art with its 17 shelters and over 4000 individual Rock Paintings. As recently as 1926 a farmer found in Eland Cave a Bushman's bow and quiver together with other personal items. He also noticed there was freshly-cut grass spread out to sleep on: Is it possible that Bushmen could have lived here as recently as this . . . ?

Between the years 1929 and 1943 this region saw the beginnings of four hotels: These came into existence on lands that had once been established farms.

Most of this region's foothills and upper escarpment are administered by the Department of Forestry and a permit is required when walking through this area. Perhaps the most popular walk is to the Sterkspruit Falls, beneath Cathkin Peak, and upstream there are several delightful spots for swimming and admiring the view.

Another enjoyable walk, is up to the Sphinx – which takes one through indigenous forests and cascading waterfalls to this weathered sandstone form which roughly resembles its strange counterpart in Egypt.

From here more waterfalls, especially in summer, can be seen, plunging down the 'Little Berg'. One will also be able to see 'Gatberg' – known to the Zulus as Intunja (the eye of a needle) a small mountain with a hole through it, and situated at the lower end of the 'Dragon's Back'.

There are many other scenic walks in the area, details of which are available at the respective resorts.

Mountains of Mystery...

Whenever in the midst of these dominant bastions one senses that haunting aura, and the fascination of the unknown: A wonderment of forgotten stories that must remain forever untold – casting their mystic spell on these "Dragon Mountains".

What admirable names the summits of the Champagne/Cathkin region have! "Sterkhorn" named after the boisterous Sterkspruit – strong, flowing stream. "Champagne Castle" where Major Grantham's batman inadvertently 'cracked the bottle' in early anticipation of success during that first ascent of the peak. "Cathkin Peak" named after the bonnie braes (slopes) near Scotland's Glasgow. "Monk's Cowl" where one can discern in its brooding silhouette the hooded cleric that surely frequents this sceptred cloister of spires.

Champagne Castle Hotel

★★TYYY

The Drakensberg resort nearest to the country's highest peaks and finest mountain scenery. Accommodation consists of cottages, rondavels and family units – all en-suite, and each with wall-to-wall carpeting, radio and phone. This friendly hotel provides good fare, organised entertainment, walks, climbs and horse-riding etc.

Telex No: 625385
Write to: Private Bag X8, Winterton 3340, Natal.
Telephone: (03642) and ask for Champagne Castle.

CAYLEY GUEST LODGE

'Highlands Hospitality in the Natal Drakensberg'

Overlooking Champagne Castle and Cathkin Peak – this Family 'Berg Resort offers superb country-style cooking; and has every amenity for you to enjoy a wonderful holiday amidst the splendour of majestic mountain scenery; and in the happy gathering of new-found friends. Your hosts – the Diack family.

Write to: P.O. Box 241, Winterton 3340, or Phone us at: (03682) and ask for 2722.

EL MIRADOR

★T

For homely comfort, friendly atmosphere and country-style cooking: This family Hotel is pleasantly placed in the Drakensberg's picturesque foothills – has all sporting and indoor activities – and the resort's mini-bus takes you into the very heart of the 'berg to view the region's many scenic attractions. We are also well-equipped for business conferences, seminars and weddings.

Write to: Private Bag X9, Winterton, Natal 3340.
Telephone: (03642) and ask for El Mirador.

CATHKIN PARK HOTEL

★TYYY

Nestled in the rolling hills of the Natal Drakensberg – you'll come alive in this fresh mountain air. Cathkin offers comfortable accommodation, a warm sense of belonging, good country cooking, log fires in winter, tennis, swimming, bowls, excellent horse-riding, hiking and indoor recreation. Golf, squash, water sports and trout fishing can be arranged. Children are most welcome.

Telephone: (03642) ask for Cathkin No. 1 or write to: Cathkin Park Hotel, Private Bag X12, Winterton 3340. Telex No. S.A. 6-46036.

The Nest Hotel

★TYYY

Beautifully situated in the very heart of the Drakensberg, The Nest Hotel is readily accessible on tarred roads from Johannesburg, on the N3 route, through Harrismith ... and then via Oliviershoek Pass and Winterton: Or from Durban on the N3 – take Central Berg Resorts/Loskop turnoff. Facilities include an informal Ladies Bar, bowling greens, tennis courts, riding and golf course nearby.

Telephone: (03642) and ask for Nest 2, or – Write to: Private Bag X14, Winterton 3340; or Telex: S.A. 6-28231.

DRAGON PEAKS CARAVAN PARK

The Caravaners, Campers and Cottage Resort in the heart of the mountains near Champagne Castle that offers you all holiday resort facilities.

Write to: Dragon Peaks Holiday Resort. P.O. Winterton Natal 3340. Telephone us at (03642) and ask for Dragon Peaks No. 1.

MOUNTAIN SPLENDOUR CARAVAN PARK

Situated on a farm with magnificent views of Champagne Castle and Cathkin Peak. A clean, well-maintained park with spacious lawns, and a swimming pool.

Write: Private Bag X23, Winterton 3340.
Telephone: (03682) 3503.

INJASUTI

CHAMPAGNE CASTLE 3377m
MONK'S COWL CAVE
MONK'S COWL 3234m
SOUTH GULLY
CATHKIN PEAK 3149m

This is perhaps the most dramatically beautiful and unspoilt region of the entire Drakensberg. The hutted camp has a magnificent outlook onto the south-eastern slopes of Champagne Castle, Monk's Cowl and Cathkin Peak – with the eNjasuthi Buttress (3202 m) and the heights of the Trojan Wall peering down from the west. This resort can lay claim to being the nearest to the highest peaks in the 'berg, with Mafadi (3446 m) and the eNjasuthi Dome at 3410 metres being the highest peaks in South Africa. The aerial picture shows The Triplets – with the Eastern Triplet (3143 m) in the foreground and the Western Triplet (3187 m) directly behind it – being rated as one of the most dangerous climbs in the 'berg, and was only first climbed in 1951. The eNjasuthi Buttress (3202 m) can be seen in the right background.

Until recently (1963) this resort had been a cattle farm – with Tiny and Pat Harries taking it over to establish a 'berg holiday resort. After seventeen years of wonderful mountain life – and battling with a long stretch of access road that had to be maintained by them, they finally accepted an 'offer to buy' from the Natal Parks Board in 1980 – and 'Solitude' then became 'Injasuti'. The resort has the beautiful eNjasuthi River – which tumbles through a magnificent gorge – with waterfalls and large rock pools.

The upper foothills have a great number of rock shelters in the sandstone cliffs – and must have been a paradise for the Bushmen cave dwellers. 'Battle Cave' has a series of well-preserved rock paintings where a group of Bushmen are depicted – engaged in battle with another tribe.

... Bushmen hunters have long since departed, but these beautiful surroundings remain for all to appreciate, today.

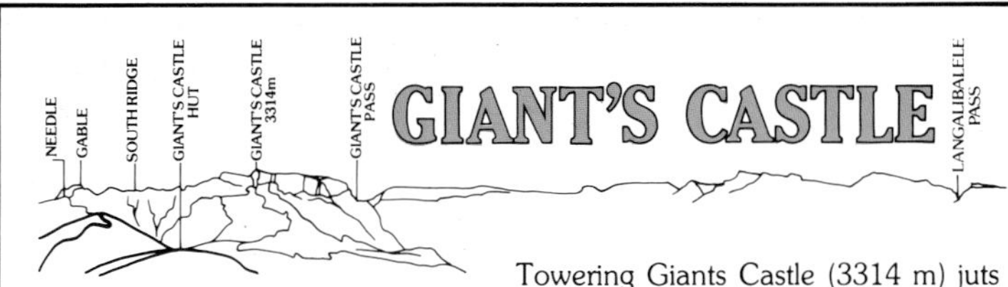

GIANT'S CASTLE

Towering Giants Castle (3314 m) juts out 3 km from 'Long Wall' and the 'berg escarpment, to dominate cliffs and plains of the Little Berg. These prominent heights have witnessed many stirring events in the annals of history.

Apart from retaliatory skirmishes between Bushmen and settlers of Natal in the 1860's, the area was also the scene of an unfortunate incident... when an Amahlubi chief Langalibalele and his warriors fought a detachment of men, commanded by Col. Durnford, at the top of what is today Langalibalele Pass. Prior to this engagement... diamonds had been discovered in 1870 at Kimberley: And many of Langalibalele's men working in those diggings preferred their payment in guns rather than in cash. The arming of these Amahlubi tribesmen worried the colonial government who ordered their weapons to be handed in to the authorities for registration. This order was subsequently rejected and after further ultimatums, and much unpleasantness, Langalibalele and his followers trekked over the 'berg at Giant's Castle...

Col. Durnford, who had been sent after Langalibalele, intercepted the warriors' rearguard at the top of a mountain pass near Giant's Castle. There, negotiations broke down: Facing many thousand hostile tribesmen, and no prearranged support forthcoming... with bullets and spears raining upon them, Durnford and his men, leaving the fallen, were forced into disorderly retreat.

In 1874, a year after the rebellion, soldiers from the 75th Regiment camped beneath the 'Main Caves', whilst stationed there to destroy the 'berg passes in an effort to prevent the Bushmen cattle raiders from escaping over the escarpment, with herds of stolen stock.

Today, Giant's Castle is very much more peaceful. The Natal Parks Board took over the reserve in 1903 at a time when there were only about 200 Eland in existence in all of Natal. The Eland is now no longer an endangered species and shares its mountain home with the abundant wildlife of the reserve.

Giant's Castle is well-known for its realistic Bushman cave museum – where lifelike Bushmen figures, bring alive scenes of an era past.

This region has many fine caves and paintings, the beautiful Bushman's River, and a variety of walks through expansive unspoilt surroundings.

Giant's Castle

LOTENI

THE HAWK 3177m
EAGLE
THE TENT 3130m
LOTENI NATURE RESERVE
PITOLI
GIANT'S CASTLE

The huge rock walls of Giant's Castle (3314 m), one of the highest mountains in the Drakensberg range, sheer off to the east from the roughly north-south running main 'berg – to form what is often called the 'Giant's Ridge'. The hutted camp of Loteni faces these heights from the south – and in winter the shadowed south-facing slopes of the Giant, being protected from the sun, are often covered in snow for several weeks at a time.

Like many of the 'berg resorts, Loteni was also once a farm; owned by the Root family – with Peter Root a descendent of the early settlers, later becoming the Senior Ranger (now retired) when the Natal Parks Board purchased the property. The original cottages of the Root family (1905) – and a settlers' museum of interesting items, can be seen near the entrance to the reserve.

Loteni Nature Reserve – like Giant's Castle Game Reserve, also has a large number of wildlife including the Eland, Grey Rhebuck, Mountain Reedbuck, Duiker, Oribi and Bushbuck. The swift-flowing Loteni River is well-stocked with trout, and there are numerous pleasant walks in the reserve.

Vergelegen – This small Parks Board Nature Reserve is situated in the beautiful upper reaches of the Umkomaas River (see picture bottom right). The highest mountain south of Kilamanjaro (Thabana Nylenyana 3482 m), only 36 m higher than Mafadi at Injasuti, is situated just over the escarpment.

Kamberg – Situated near the head waters of the Mooi River, this nature reserve is most popular with trout fishermen. There is also a large trout hatchery here. The walks are most interesting and there are some fine examples of Bushman paintings in this Little Berg area.

CHACMA BABOON (Papio ursinus); Seen with their young, in mountainous regions in most of the reserves.

HYRAX – Rock Dassie – (Procavia capensis): Usually sun themselves on rock ledges.

KLIPSPRINGER (Oreotragus oreotragus): Occur mainly on rock-strewn slopes of the High Berg.

BUSHBUCK (Tragelaphus scriptus): Seldom seen, since they prefer dense bush and forests.

MOUNTAIN REEDBUCK (Redunca fulvorufula): Can be found from river valleys to the Lesotho plateau.

FAUNA AND FLORA

Wildlife of the Drakensberg is usually found within those areas where vegetation and climate is most suitable to that particular species.
Eland – largest of the antelope, can usually be seen in the foothills of the Little Berg; whilst the smaller Mountain Reedbuck prefers the warm slopes of the sandstone cliffs, and its protea savannah. The Grey Rhebuck and tiny Grey Duiker are perhaps the commonest antelope to be sighted. Some animals, like the Klipspringer, often remain in certain areas where there is an abundance of rock-strewn boulders... whereas the Cape Bushbuck, though rarely seen, is usually content to graze in yellowwood forests or densely-wooded ravines.
Some animals almost became extinct – but due to careful conservation are now increasing in numbers: Amongst these are the Eland; the Red Hartebeest; and the Black Wildebeest.
There are animals that make strange sounds when surprised – such as the 'sneezing' of the inquisitive Blesbok; the piercing whistle of the Southern Reedbuck; and the almost quiet whistle of the Oribi as it resorts to crouching low in tall grass to escape being seen.

Birds also have their preferred regions. Lammergeyers, Cape Vultures, and Black Eagles wheel majestically in the winds of the High Berg, whereas the Jackal Buzzards and Martial Eagles frequent rocky outcrops of the open grasslands of the Little Berg.

JACKAL BUZZARD (Buteo rufofuscus): Birds of prey of the High Berg, and also of the open grasslands.

BLACK EAGLE (Aquila verreauxi) and CAPE VULTURE (Gyps coprotheres) fighting over a carcass.

ELAND (Taurotragus oryx): At 650 kg and 170 cm high – largest of all the antelopes and extremely agile.

REEDBUCK (Redunca arundinum): Found among the tall grasses and reeds of the Little Berg.

FLORA...

The vegetation of the Drakensberg is predominantly determined by altitude, and the plant's growing position – either on the sunny north-facing slopes, or the wetter and cooler south-facing hillsides.
At lower altitudes one finds an abundance of grasslands with some forest. Moving higher, the drier hills and slopes are often covered with Protea – and during September the red flowering Mountain Bottlebrush blooms.
Higher up, one reaches the 'Alpine' conditions of the Lesotho plateau; and the High Berg where Ericas and 'everlastings' flourish in the bleaker conditions.
During late spring wild flowers such as the Blue Agapanthus, Pink Dieramas, and Fire Lilies can all be seen at their best.

GREATER DOUBLE-COLLARED SUNBIRD: The Cinnyris afer afer can always be seen near flowers.

PROTEA KAFFRA: The Drakensberg Protea blooms on a small tree of some 3,7 m high.

MOUNTAIN BOTTLEBRUSH (Greyia sutherlandii): A hardy small tree with vivid scarlet blooms.

HELICHRYSUM: "Everlasting", like the H. sesamoides, are hardy perennials found on mountain slopes.

DIERAMA IGNEUM: Small pink harebells found in the 'berg; and from the East Cape to the Transvaal.

Mountain sunset from 'Tree Fern' Cave.

Above: Trail riders with Giant's Castle in the background. 'Tree Fern' Cave (below) overlooks the beautiful eNjasuthi Valley and is usually the first night's stop-over point.

HORSE TRAILS FROM HILLSIDE CAMP

Several years ago it was decided by the Natal Parks Board to curb horse-riding in the higher regions of the 'berg where horse trails that were regularly traversing the same paths were indirectly causing extensive soil erosion. Horse trails from Hillside camp, near Giant's Castle, thus came into being – when rides into the 'berg could be better controlled and organized.

Upon prior arrangement, trails of up to four days can be undertaken – with an experienced Parks Board Ranger who will lead the way and point out the many interesting features of fauna, flora and items of historical interest.

One carries ones own food and clothing in saddle-bags – and nights are often spent in the 'luxury' of Tree Fern Cave, or 'Fergie's Cave.' A packhorse is used to carry firewood and bedding rolls for the longer trails. There are shorter rides of 2 days (with an overnight stay in Tree Fern Cave) and also one day, and half day rides that can be undertaken.

A TEST FOR MAN, MULE AND MACHINE!

Sani Pass is the only road access to the Kingdom of Lesotho from the east. The steep and tortuous 8 – 12 km mountain roadway commences from the South African Police Post at the Natal border and winds and zig-zags its way to the summit, and Lesotho border, near the edge of the escarpment: From here the 'road' traverses Black Mountain Pass – and continues along the rough tracks to Mokhotlong which was once a very remote settlement whose only contact with the outside world was by mule train along this important and well-used trail.
The Pass which can only be negotiated by 4-wheel drive vehicles started its life as a mountain path for the San people (Bushmen) and later for herdsmen and their goods. In the 1930's the trail was improved to that of a 'Bridle Path' and was used by mules and packhorses to carry their loads into the interior. Trade was thus established by the Basutoland Government, with South Africa – grain and essential foods being taken up the pass . . . and mule trains coming down the steep and stony gradients heavily laden with ox-hides and mohair skins.
Further improvements were made to this trail and the first 4-wheel drive vehicle managed to negotiate the pass and reach the summit in 1949. The widening and laying down of concrete strips together with the 'rounding' of many of the sharper bends has made the test of man, mule and machine that much easier; yet it still remains an exciting experience for the adventurous many who take this jeep ride to the 'Roof of Africa'.

(Top left) Heated engines cool whilst visitors to the top of the pass alight to admire the superb views.
(Bottom left) Winter snows at Sani Pass – between the high spurs of Phinong and Sakeng.
(Left) Snowfalls can be heavy. A Land Rover comes to a stand-still in a deep drift.
(Bottom right) Spectacular grandeur of a dramatic mountain countryside.

SANI PASS

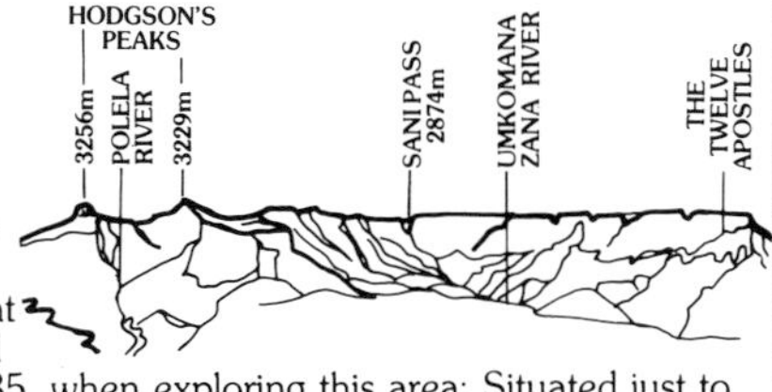

The predominant mountains of this region are the twin Hodgson's Peaks (3256 m) which with their shape of a 'giant's cup' are easily recognisable from a great distance . . . and were aptly named by Alan Francis Gardiner, in 1835, when exploring this area: Situated just to the south of the Sani Pass, these peaks acquired their existing name in 1862, when, whilst searching for a group of cattle-marauding Bushmen raiders on top of the escarpment, Thomas Hodgson, who was a member of the commando in pursuit, was accidentally mortally wounded in the thigh by one of his comrades when firing at a young Bushman on horseback trying to make a getaway.

Today the only evidence that the Bushmen existed are their rock paintings in the area – with those at Ikanti Shelter being some of the clearest in the 'berg. At another nearby shelter carbon-dating processes, have proved that there were cave dwellers in the vicinity some 7600 years ago!
Ikanti Mountain, directly across the Umkomanayana River, from the hotel, has the unusual formations of 'Balancing Rock' and 'Napoleon's Hat' which is an interesting climb of about 2½ hours duration.
The region adjoins forestry reserve; with Eland and smaller buck inhabiting the rugged surrounding foothills.

Sani Pass owes its existence to the little San people who were the first to 'open up' this route: Where once they had scrambled over rocky boulders and heath... today one wonders what the future has in store for this historic and challenging mountain pass.

The Umkomanayana River which flows down from the slopes of Hodgson's Peaks is well-stocked with Brown Trout – and the waterfall, a short walk from the hotel is a popular attraction.

DRAKENSBERG GARDEN REGION

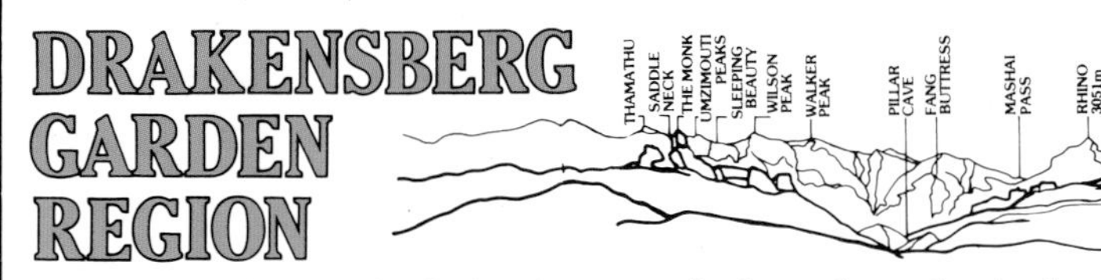

The southern slopes of the Drakensberg were the first to be explored, when Alan Francis Gardiner made a journey to this region in 1835, whilst attempting to find an overland route to the Cape . . . years later the first settlers were to arrive in the area in 1886.

The Rhino (3051 m) is the most impressive peak here, and with its upturned 'horn' is easily identifiable. A climb to its summit is accomplished by scrambling up the Mashai Pass. The rich indigenous vegetation seen here, and the towering sandstone forms makes this pass one of the more interesting in the 'berg. Walker (3322 m), and Wilson Peaks (3342 m) are the highest points to the left of the pass – and were presumably named after early settlers. The Drakensberg Garden Hotel was established on the upper reaches of the Umzimkulu River by the Stiebel family in 1935: They chose a wonderful site – though in those days it was extremely inaccessible, especially during bad weather. In its lovely setting with wide unobstructed views of the Drakensberg, and its dramatic weather-worn foothills, the area is richly endowed with the natural attractions of the southern 'berg region.

The southern 'berg is well-known for its trout fishing; with the waters of the Umzimkulu and Mlambonja rivers – and the many dams in the area, providing challenging sport. The rivers are stocked with brown trout and most of the dams also have black bass.

All the valleys that lead up to the high 'berg in this region are most spectacular: Pillar Cave (left) is situated in the Mashai Valley, and 'Sleeping Beauty Valley', next to it, has impressive rock formations such as the clearly defined 'Monk' – and the large Sleeping Beauty Cave.

BUSHMAN'S NEK

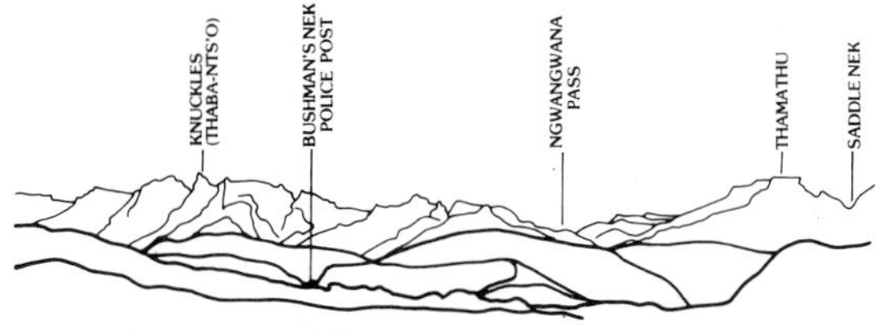

This is the southern-most 'berg resort region of the Natal Drakensberg and has a completely different character to that of the central and northern 'berg. The area is less populated and its many well-kept farms extend right into the foothills, to meet the forestry reserve lands.

Receiving better rainfalls than the northern Drakensberg, the mountain slopes feed many rivers and streams that flow swift and clear throughout the year... over worn bolders and smooth sandstone beds: With long stretches of river, easily accessible – and with grassy banks, this is certainly a fly-fisherman's dream.

The Ngwangwana River flows past the Bushman's Nek Hotel and continues on into the Coleford Nature Reserve, another popular venue amongst trout fishermen. There is a police post at the Bushman's Nek border and passport holders may cross over to the bridle path on the Lesotho side.

After the Devil's Knuckles, the Drakensberg gradually reverts to "Little 'Berg"... which then extends through to the Eastern Cape's highlands.

There are also many rock shelters with Bushmen paintings to be admired in this area of the southern 'berg.

Timeless Tranquility

After a flurry of falling snow has drifted among cloud-covered peaks, the quietness of this countryside is coldly reflected in the mirrored sheen of a meandering river: Soon shadows will gradually drape these slopes and fields as the gleam of day merges, almost reluctantly, into the dimming shades of dusk.

Day's end in the 'berg ... ecstatic moments of solitude and contentment that must have been enjoyed by the little Bushmen in their rock shelters above the valleys... by African tribes resting outside reed huts as a fire's glow warms the evening meal... and by intrepid settlers and their families relaxing contentedly on a homely 'stoep' – pondering on doubts of the morrow.

Today, the majestic grandeur of the dauntless Drakensberg, with its capricious moods, is there to be admired by those who can appreciate such magnificence in all its guises of colour and clime: Hopefully none will ever subscribe to the view that such scenes can be improved upon by progress, development and change – for these mountains have been revered and cherished through an eventful past... to the challenging present... and will endure into the unknown future.

Sotho hunters on Cleft Peak (3281 m)